Self Esteem

Are We Really Better Than We Think?

DAVID M. TYLER

Introduction

Over the past 40 years the idea of esteeming one's self has had a tremendous influence on the Christian church. Years ago the pursuit of self love was generally thought to be sinful. Self-esteem is not a biblical concept, and in fact, the opposite is true. Scripture teaches that we are to esteem others as greater than ourselves. However, since the 1970's Christians have been encouraged to develop a "healthy" self-esteem. Beloved Christian authors have warned that a negative self image is the basis of nearly all psychological problems and it even leads to sinful behavior. It is the proposed answer to nearly all problems of living. As you read this booklet you will see that Archie's story is common to many. Certainly everyone has periods of self-doubt and discouragement about circumstances in their lives.

The truth is that we have too much self-esteem and not enough God-esteem (i.e. worship, adoration, obedience, holiness, love for God and others). Ultimately, we must view ourselves as God does, as sinners, desperately in need of God's forgiving, pardoning, enabling grace and love. When we truly see how wretched we are, we then can fully embrace His pardon, forgiveness, and grace. We can see ourselves as His children and part of His kingdom and therefore work for His purposes in the world. This doesn't mean we're more valuable or have better self-esteem, but that we realize it isn't about us—it's about God.

Self-Esteem: Are We Better Than We Think?

Archie's life has been one problem after another. His parents divorced when he was 10 years old. His father was verbally abusive to Archie and his mother. He never had many friends in school and often felt lonely. Archie thought things would get better after he got married, but things did not change very much. He and his wife have been having marital problems for the past six years. Archie maintains he has always felt inferior.

Archie's wife, Edith, told him that he has no self-esteem. She asked him how he could expect anyone to love him if he didn't love himself. Archie decided that maybe he needed to learn to love himself so he could have normal relationships and a happy life. He bought some self-help books that promised to improve his self-esteem.

Like so many people today, Archie now believes he is a better person than he thought he was. Dozens of prominent Christian authors assure Archie that the haunting feelings of guilt, shame, unworthiness, and not being "good enough" are false. They assure Archie that he is competent, adequate, and special, worthy of Christ dying for him, significant and okay. Archie has learned a lot about the nature of man. Archie now believes that:

- Self-esteem is a vital element of human personality.
- Self-esteem is a feeling and not a thought process.

- Being mistreated by others can cause a person's self-image to deteriorate and/or not develop properly.
- Self-love is a prerequisite to being loved by others and loving others, including God.
- A person must fix his poor self-image.

But is Archie really better than he thinks?

Archie and Edith serve the Lord at a nearby Baptist church. Archie is a deacon and Edith teaches a ladies' Sunday school class. They met while they were attending a Bible college in the Midwest. Archie believes in the inerrancy of God's Word and is very strong in his faith. However, when it comes to solving life's problems, Archie has very few skills.

Like many Christians today, Archie looks for answers outside of the Scripture. He looks to psychology for instruction and help. Psychology tells Archie he needs to love himself.

In Genesis 3:1-5, we have the first theological conversation ever recorded. The Serpent promised Eve her eyes would be opened if she ate from the forbidden tree. Nothing would be hidden from her. She would understand the deep things of God. **"You will be like God,"** he said. The Serpent further encouraged her to defy God's command with, **"You will not surely die."** Self-exaltation is rebellion against God. Eve's desire to worship God became a lust to be God and worship self.

The natural tendency of all men is to throw off the restraints of humanity and become God. This affinity for self, for godhood, has grieved godly men and women down through the years. For example, in 1898, Andrew Murray wrote: "the one real hindrance to this life of the Spirit is the power of our evil self."[1]

In 1945, L.E. Maxwell wrote: "Self has usurped the throne ... Self is the new and false center upon which man has fixed."[2] Puritan Octavius Winslow wrote: "Self must be mortally wounded before Christ lives in us. The two sovereigns cannot reign at the same time and upon the same throne... In proportion as Christ lives in us, Self dies!"[3]

Thomas Brooks wrote: "Self seeking *blinds* the soul ... There is not a greater hindrance to all the duties of piety than self seeking."[4] And John Calvin wrote: "... For, such is the blindness with which we all rush into self love that each one of us seems to himself to have just cause to be proud of himself and to despise all others in comparison. ... There is no other remedy than to tear out from our inward parts this most deadly pestilence of love of strife and love of self."[5]

Most importantly, the Apostle Paul, under inspiration of the Holy Spirit, wrote: **"For the flesh sets its desire against the Spirit, and the Spirit against the flesh; for these are in opposition to one another"** (Galatians 5:17). They all wrote about the same thing. They wrote about the struggle in their life between God and self.

[1] Andrew Murray in William Law, *Freedom From a Self-Centered Life / Dying to Self* (Minneapolis: Bethany House Publishers, 1977), p. 6.
[2] L.E. Maxwell, *Born Crucified* (Chicago: Moody Press, 1973), p. 56.
[3] Octavius Winslow, "The Lights and Shadows of Spiritual Life", Grace Gems, 2002.
[4] Thomas Brooks, *Precious Remedies Against Satan's Devices* (Carlisle, Pa.: The Banner of Truth, 1968), p. 189.
[5] John T. McNeill, *Calvin: Institutes of the Christian Religion* (Philadelphia: The Westminster Press, 1960, Vol. 1), pp. 691, 694, (Institutes 3.7.2,4).

There is a struggle in the life of every believer to keep God on the throne of his heart. It is difficult because the heart of man is constantly and relentlessly trying to dethrone God and enthrone self. Trying to keep God on the throne of one's heart is like a tug-of-war. It is the flesh warring against the Spirit, and the Spirit against the flesh. The believer says in his heart, "I want God on the throne. I want self on the throne. God. Self. God. Self."

The attraction, the lure to be God is present in every man's heart. Isaiah encapsulated this when he wrote: **"All we like sheep have gone astray; we have turned, every one, to his *own* way"** (Isaiah 53:6 NKJV, italics mine).

Isaiah wrote about Lucifer's desire to be God: **"But you said in your heart, 'I will ascend to heaven; I will raise my throne above the stars of God, and I will sit on the mount of assembly... I will ascend above the heights of the clouds; I will make myself like the Most High'"** (Isaiah 14:13, 14). The Serpent knew Eve could not resist the appeal of self-exaltation. We, the offspring of Adam and Eve cannot resist it either. We are idolaters. We are self-worshippers. John Calvin wrote, "we may gather that man's nature, so to speak, is a perpetual factory of idols."[6]

1. THE PRESENTATION PROBLEM

Finally, Archie became so unhappy that he decided to seek professional help. Let's go along with Archie and see how a biblical counselor can help him discover God's truth in his personal life. The counselor explained

---

[6] Calvin: *Institutes of the Christian Religion*, op. cit., Vol. 1, p. 108, (Institutes 1.11.8).

that there are three problem levels they would explore together.[7] First is the presentation problem. The presentation problem identifies what Archie *thinks* is the problem. When the counselor asks Archie why he came for counseling, his answer is called the presentation problem. It is what Archie says he is feeling at the moment. For example, Archie might have said he is depressed, fearful, or anxious. But Archie said his reason for coming to counseling was that he has a problem with low self-esteem. He sees himself as completely defeated and without hope. Archie feels doomed to a life of frustration and despair. In many cases the presentation problem is not the cause of the counselee's problem, but an effect or symptom of the real problem.

The prophet Ezekiel wrote: **"You will loathe yourselves in your own sight for all the evil things that you have done"** (Ezekiel 20:43). When a person complains that he hates himself, or has low self-esteem, a wise counselor will look for sinful habits of behavior. People do not hate themselves. People hate their circumstances and their behaviors that led to those circumstances. Self-love is universal. Paul wrote: **"No one ever hated his own flesh, but nourishes and cherishes it"** (Ephesians 5:29). If Archie truly hated himself he would not want things to be better, but worse. If you hate someone you don't want good things to happen to them, but evil things. You hope they break their leg, but you don't hope they win the lottery. Archie values himself. Archie sees himself as a victim and feels that others have mistreated him. Archie's attitude is that others have been insensitive and uncaring toward him. They have not understood him. They have been unfair. Archie feels he deserves better

---

[7] For a more detailed explanation on the three dimensions of problems, read Jay Adams' book, *Competent to Counsel.*

treatment. You can see that Archie actually nourishes and cherishes himself.

2. THE PERFORMACE PROBLEM

The performance problem is a specific behavior that is the cause of the counselee's problem. In Archie's case the performance problem is the way he is performing or behaving in response to life's difficulties. At this point the counselor will begin to gather data from Archie.[8] He will ask specific questions, exploring systematically all areas and relationships in Archie's life. A counselor must probe pointedly and lovingly into areas of family, church, friends, social activities, marriage, sex, finances, and work. One of Archie's problems is his bad temper.

People feel badly because of bad behavior. The relationship between feelings and behavior is taught throughout the Bible. Ezekiel said people who behave sinfully will loathe themselves (Ezekiel 20:43). The book of Proverbs clearly teaches that feelings flow from behavior. For example:

> **My son, give attention to my words; incline your ear to my sayings. Do not let them depart from your sight; keep them in the midst of your heart. For they are life to those who find them, and health to all their body** (Proverbs 4:20-22).

David understood well the connection between behavior and feelings when he wrote:

---

[8] Data gathering is an essential part of understanding the counselee's problems and how to help him. For more information on how to gather data, read chapter twenty-five of *Competent to Counsel*, by Jay Adams.

> **There is no soundness in my flesh because of Your indignation; there is no health in my bones because of my sin. For my iniquities are gone over my head; as a heavy burden they weigh too much for me. My wounds grow foul and fester because of my folly** (Psalm 38:3-5).

Peter, quoting Psalm 34:12-13, points out that good living produces good feelings:

> **For, "He who would love life and see good days, let him refrain his tongue from evil and his lips from speaking deceit"** (1 Peter 3:10 NKJV).

The correlation between feelings and behavior is seen in David's son Amnon and his sinful desires for his half-sister Tamar:

> **Now it was after this that Absalom the son of David had a beautiful sister whose name was Tamar, and Amnon the son of David loved her. Amnon was so frustrated because of his sister Tamar that he made himself ill, for she was a virgin, and it seemed hard to Amnon to do anything to her** (2 Samuel 13:1-2).

Peter speaks of the importance of good behavior to a good conscience when he wrote:

> **...and keep a good conscience so that in the thing in which you are slandered,**

those who revile your good behavior in Christ will be put to shame (1 Peter 3:16).

When man sins he feels it. Jay Adams wrote:

> A good conscience, according to Peter, depends upon good behavior. Good lives come from good deeds; good consciences come from good behavior. Conscience, which is man's ability to evaluate his own actions, activates unpleasant visceral and other bodily warning devices when he sins. … These responses serve to alert him to the need for correction of the wrong behavior which the conscience would not tolerate. Bad feelings are the red light on the dashboard flashing out at us, the siren screaming at high pitch, the flag waving in front of our faces. Visceral discomfort is a God-structured means of telling human beings that they have violated their standards.[9]

3. THE PRECONDITIONING PROBLEM

The third problem is called the preconditioning problem. It is the habitual sinful response of the counselee to specific stimuli. Because of Archie's past activity he has programmed himself to respond to difficulties in the same way. For example, he has repeatedly responded to problems by blowing up and becoming angry. As a result of his explosive temper others, not wanting set him off, give in to his demands. The outcome is that he behaves

---

[9] Jay Adams, *Competent to Counsel* (Grand Rapids: Zondervan Publishing House, 1970), p. 94.

the same way in other situations, for example, at work. Archie has been disciplined on several occasions for losing his temper with co-workers. The preconditioning problem is the sinful pattern or habit that over a period of time has been established by Archie. The preconditioning problem is the underlying cause of his problem.

Beginning with the presupposition that bad feelings follow *sinful* behavior (performance problem) we can look for *patterns* of sinful behavior (preconditioning problem) in Archie's life. Keeping Ezekiel's words in mind (Ezekiel 20:43), patterns begin to emerge in Archie's behavior. Archie has a volatile temper. He even describes himself as having a "short fuse." As we continue to collect data, it becomes apparent that his temper has been a major problem in his previous two marriages.

Archie's troubles are not the result of self-hatred and low self-esteem, but his sinful behavior and attitudes. Sinners prefer themselves over others and over God (universal self-love). A study of Archie's life reveals sinful patterns and habits. Archie has been fired twice for quarreling with his superior and quit three other jobs because he believed he was not being treated fairly. When Archie started counseling, he had not worked for over a year. He admitted to anger, bitterness, envy, marital discord, and money problems.

Archie's sinful behavior and attitude result in feelings of guilt. Archie feels badly about himself. Archie should feel bad. Ezekiel said that people loathe themselves because of their sinful behavior (Ezekiel 20:43). People, like Archie, whose lives have been disrupted by feelings of guilt are referred to counselors who help them build their self-esteem. Low self-esteem is a euphemism for guilt. James Dobson says that low self-esteem leads to all kinds of sinful behavior such as "neuroticism, hatred, alcoholism, drug abuse, violence, and social disorder."[10] In other words, low self-esteem leads to sin, and therefore, nurturing self-esteem leads to righteousness.

Unlike Scripture, nowhere in psychology is the wicked heart mentioned (Jeremiah 17:9). Nowhere is sin, the cross, the Holy Spirit, and progressive sanctification mentioned. Sin produces guilt, which is reinterpreted or redefined as low self-esteem. John MacArthur wrote: "Our culture has declared war on guilt. ... No one, after all, is supposed to feel guilty. Guilt is not conducive to dignity and self-esteem. Society encourages sin, but it will not tolerate the guilt sin produces."[11]

SANCTIFICATION

> **For this is the will of God, your sanctification...** (1 Thessalonians 4:3).

> **For God has not called us for the purpose of impurity, but in sanctification** (1 Thessalonians 4:7).

The goal of all Christian counseling is sanctification. Sanctification and counseling are intimately related. There are times when a believer needs the assistance of another believer in order to effect change that pleases God. God wants Archie to change. It is a considerable change brought about by the ministry of the Word and

---

[10] James Dobson, *Hide and Seek* (Grand Rapids: Flemming H. Revell, 1979), p. 21.

[11] John F. MacArthur, Jr., *The Vanishing Conscience* (Dallas: Word Publishing Company, 1994), p. 19.

the power of the Holy Spirit. It is a change toward God.[12] It is a change that brings Archie closer to the likeness of Christ. It glorifies God. In many instances sanctification is halted and can only proceed by effective biblical counseling.

Sanctification is concerned with the putting away of sinful habits. Sin's hold over a Christian's body is not absolute. The tyranny of sin has been abolished. The Christian is a new creature with a new heart. He has died to sin. Sin is no longer the chief characteristic of his life. The believer does not have to be a slave to sin as he once was. Even so, sinful habits still persist in every Christian. They persist even to the extent that there are times when sin appears to dominate the Christian's life completely. Progressive sanctification is the process whereby these habits are put off and replaced by new righteous habits.

Sanctification is the work of God in the believer's life. It is progressive and it is a life-long process. There are three forces at work in the process of sanctification. Those forces are the Holy Spirit, God's Word, and the regenerated believer. It is a divine and human activity. Man is not passive. The Holy Spirit works, but he makes the Christian work too. The Spirit's work incites the believer to work. Paul said: **"For it is God who is at work in you, both to will and to work for His good pleasure"** (Philippians 2:13). Once again Paul said that he **"labors,"** but at the same time it is God's **"power which mightily works within me"** (Colossians 1:28-29).

---

[12] There is no such thing as change that is neutral. A person is either moving toward or away from God.

It is not an easy process. The old self is still present in the believer. It takes a great effort to put off the old self and its sinful habits and put on the new self. Change is hard, but not impossible. Consistent effort and self-control must be exercised if spiritual progress is to be made. The believer's union with Christ makes possible the putting away of the **"body of sin** (i.e., sinful habits that are in the body) **that we should no longer be slaves to sin"** (Romans 6:6 NKJV). The Christian can become cleaner, purer, and holier.

SANCTIFIED BY SELF-ESTEEM?

Christian self-esteem advocates say that self-esteem is the road to sanctification and godliness. The way to put off sin is to put on a "healthy" self-image. Josh McDowell's words are representative of Christian self-theorists: "A healthy sense of self-worth is fundamental in drawing us closer to God."[13] This idea permeates "Christian" psychology.

James Dobson attributes all sorts of sinful behavior to low self-esteem. For example, in his book, *Hide and Seek*, Dobson wrote:

> The health of an entire society depends on the ease with which its individual members can gain personal acceptance. Thus, whenever the keys of self-esteem are seemingly out of reach for a large percentage of the people, as in twentieth-century America, then widespread "mental illness," neuroticism, hatred, alcoholism, drug abuse, violence, and social disorder

---

[13] Josh McDowell, *Building Your Self-Image* (Wheaton: Tyndale House, 1978), p. 47.

will certainly occur. Personal worth is not something human beings are free to take or leave. We must have it, and when it is unattainable, everybody suffers.[14]

According to Dobson, low self-esteem is the cause of nearly all problems of life. It even leads to sinful behavior. The flip side is that self-esteem is the solution for these same sins.

Self-esteem is said to make us better people. The Christian spin is that it is fundamental to Christ-likeness or sanctification. The presuppositions of self-esteem have become so integrated into Christian thinking that to undertake criticism is to invite anger and contempt.

The solution for sin is not self-esteem. To be content with good feelings about oneself is to be blinded to the truth. It is to be content with sin. The inclination toward sin, as every Christian will testify, is not erased by becoming a believer. Christians derive a great deal of pleasure from sin—sinful pleasures so appalling and shameful, one would wonder if the person is a believer at all; sinful pleasures so deeply ingrained they battle with them for years and years.

Self-love is not a biblically legitimate goal. A Christian can only be satisfied with himself when he is in the proper relationship with Christ. Only then can he have a clear conscience before God and man. However, a believer is never fully satisfied with himself because he never achieves total and final sanctification in this life.

---

[14] James Dobson, *Hide and Seek* (Grand Rapids: Fleming H. Revell, 1994), pp. 20-21.

HOW TO HELP ARCHIE CHANGE / PUT OFF AND PUT ON

Self-love is universal. People do not hate themselves. People hate the mess, confusion, and disorder they have made of their lives as the result of their sinful responses to problems and people. The consequence is that they feel guilty. Man does not sin in a vacuum. There is an effect to sinful behavior. In our psychologized world, guilt—feeling bad about ourselves—is reinterpreted as low self-esteem.

Archie's life showed sinful patterns and habits. One sinful habit was his volatile temper. His pattern of blowing up at people resulted in marital problems, loss of friends, and loss of employment. Solomon wrote: **"A quick-tempered man acts foolishly, and a man of evil devices is hated"** (Proverbs 14:17). Archie did not have many friends. People with bad tempers seldom do. People don't like to associate with people who have bad tempers. They blurt out whatever comes to mind. They act and say foolish things they usually regret later. **"A hot-tempered man stirs up strife"** (Proverbs 15:18). His days are filled with trouble. He always has to seek someone's forgiveness. **"A fool *always* loses his temper, but a wise man holds it back"** (Proverbs 29:11, italics mine). The word "always" emphasizes the repetitiveness of his behavior. The fool always or habitually loses his temper. He needs to put on self-control and learn to "hold back" from venting and unleashing his anger on others. Archie must be taught patience and self-control.

STEP ONE: TEACHING

Archie's complaint was low self-esteem. He claimed

14

that others treated him unfairly and mean. As a result Archie has a negative self-image that hampers his relationships and keeps him from finding and holding a job.

Biblical counselors are extremely concerned with accurate doctrine. Paul exhorted Timothy to **"Retain the standard of sound words which you have heard from me, in the faith and love which are in Christ Jesus"** (2 Timothy 1:13). Whatever may happen to Timothy in his ministry, Paul warned him that it was vital that he hold fast to what Paul had taught.

God's people need to be careful because they will be tempted to give up the standard of sound words. One particular way God's people have been tempted and fallen is very cunning and crafty. Many have been tricked into believing that their doctrine is the same as some of the teachings found in humanist psychology, when in fact it is the opposite. Integrationists will assure you that self-actualization is the same as progressive sanctification. They will tell you that Freud's theory of the unconscious is synonymous with the Bible's teaching about the heart of man. It is impertinent and arrogant for man to think that he can supplement the Bible with his own ideas. Error that is mixed with truth contaminates the truth, making it error.

Man's doctrines and theories must never be the standard of sound words. No doctrine can be sound that exalts man. No system can be a standard of sound words unless it is perfectly Scriptural. To be Scriptural it must teach that God's Word is sufficient, as well as inerrant. Any doctrine which does not have the Father, Son, and Holy Spirit as equal persons is not sound. Any doctrine that does not teach that man is utterly fallen, wretched, like dust on a scale, meaningless, and an enemy to God who needs saving (Isaiah 40:15-17) is not sound. Any doctrine which gives man a nature whereby man may compliment, praise, or esteem himself is not sound.

The counselor must teach Archie doctrine if he is going to help him change. That is why the counselor must be a specialist in Bible knowledge, interpretation, and its application. He must understand what the Bible says about marriage, divorce, remarriage, depression, fear, forgiveness, bizarre behavior, church discipline, sin, guilt, self, habit, how to change, etc. His job is to teach and apply God's Word to the seemingly endless combinations of problems in Archie's life.

Understanding doctrine is the only way Archie will be able to distinguish between righteousness and sin. Many believers have so little doctrinal training that they are easily led astray into false doctrines such as selfism. The Apostle Paul warned Timothy about this when he wrote:

> **As I urged you upon my departure for Macedonia, remain on at Ephesus so that you may instruct certain men not to teach strange doctrines, nor to pay attention to myths and endless genealogies, which give rise to mere speculation rather than furthering the administration of God which is by faith** (1 Timothy 1:3-4).

Jesus said that people fall into doctrinal error because they do not know the Scriptures or the power of God (Matthew 22:29). Doctrinal error leads to all kinds of sinful behaviors and attitudes. Anger, bitterness, revenge, unfaithfulness, un-submissiveness, and immorality may be attributed to doctrinal error. Archie must be taught that the teachings of the Bible are the standard and the Holy Spirit is the power necessary for change. Counseling cannot proceed until Archie acknowledges this truth.[15]

The counselor must teach Archie the dynamics of habit. God made man with the capacity to formulate habits. If man did not have this ability then he would have to think about everything he does or says. Every action would have to be thought out and performed in a methodical, meticulous, and laborious way. The ability to create habits allows people to carry out complicated tasks comfortably and automatically. Habit allows a person to correspond with a friend without having to relearn how to write the letters of the alphabet. Habit allows people to walk, talk, and do thousands of different things and combinations of things without thinking about every detail.

Over time and by practice we become habituated to certain tasks. The writer of Hebrews wrote about habits when he said, **"But solid food is for the mature, who because of *practice* have their senses *trained* to discern good and evil"** (Hebrews 5:14, italics mine). People become habituated to many behaviors and attitudes. Peter wrote: **"Having eyes full of adultery that never cease from sin, enticing unstable souls, having a heart *trained* in greed, accursed children"** (2 Peter 2:14, italics

---

[15] It must be understood that the principles of Scripture cross all generational and cultural barriers. The book of Acts demonstrates this truth very well. The disciples went out from Jerusalem to the uttermost parts of the earth. The reason for this is that the Bible addresses man's fundamental problems. These problems have to do with sin, salvation, and sanctification.

mine). Some people are never satisfied or content. Paul said he learned how to be content. He wrote to the Philippian believers: **"Not that I speak from want, for I have *learned* to be content in whatever circumstances I am"** (Philippians 4:11, italics mine).

People who have sinful habits can change. Jeremiah wrote: **"You also can do good who are *accustomed* to doing evil"** (Jeremiah 13:23, italics mine). Paul wrote to Titus concerning believers who had been enslaved or habituated to sinful practices, but had changed. He said, **"For we also once *were* foolish ourselves, disobedient, deceived, *enslaved* to various lusts and pleasures, spending our life in malice and envy, hateful, hating one another"** (Titus 3:3, italics mine). When Paul wrote to the Corinthian believers, he reminded some of them about their past sinful practices which they had successfully put off. Paul wrote:

> **Or do you not know that the unrighteous will not inherit the kingdom of God? Do not be deceived; neither fornicators, nor idolaters, nor adulterers, nor effeminate, nor homosexuals, nor thieves, nor the covetous, nor drunkards, nor revilers, nor swindlers, will inherit the kingdom of God. Such were some of you; but you were washed, but you were sanctified, but you were justified in the name of the Lord Jesus Christ, and in the Spirit of our God** (1 Corinthians 6:9-11).

While habit, a blessing from God, makes life easier and more comfortable, habit can also be a curse. Sinful habits were the source of all of Archie's problems. Archie, like all people, had become habituated to sinful behaviors and attitudes. Sanctification involves the putting off of sinful habits and putting on the biblical alternative habits. It is putting off the deeds of the flesh and putting on the fruit of the Spirit (Galatians 5). Habits are learned ways of living, and therefore can be unlearned and replaced. Habits are formed when something is done repeatedly. Over time that thing becomes habitual.

Finally, the biblical counselor needs to teach Archie how to have hope. Biblical change cannot take place without it. Lack of hope is one problem all counselees experience. A biblical counselor will know how to apply biblical doctrines and principles to specific difficulties. Paul wrote, **"for whatever was written in earlier times was written for our instruction, so that through perseverance and the encouragement of the Scriptures we might have hope"** (Romans 15:4). The Scriptures, not psychology, are used to offer encouragement and hope. Paul continued, **"Now may the God of hope fill you with all joy and peace in believing, so that you will abound in hope by the power of the Holy Spirit"** (Romans 15:13).

STEP TWO: REBUKING

Bringing Archie to conviction of sin by rebuke, reproof, or admonition is the second step toward permanent change. Archie must acknowledge that he has failed to meet the standards of God's Word. He must understand that he has sinned. In order to honor God he must confess, repent, and seek forgiveness. Honoring and pleasing God is the goal of true Biblical counseling. Any counseling that claims to be biblical that does not have pleasing God as its goal is not biblical at all.

Many Christians do not believe that rebuke which brings a counselee to conviction of sin should be part of counseling. This attitude is inconsistent with the biblical approach to counseling, but not with the humanistic approach. Psychologist Carl Rogers' method of counseling is the preferred method taught in Christian seminaries, and therefore is practiced by many pastors and Christian layman. Rogerian counseling is non-directive and non-confrontational. It is amazing to listen to evangelical pastors talk about counseling people and not rebuking them or directing them in what they need to do. One pastor said, "I don't think you should tell a person what to do. I think you should just listen and help them to arrive at answers on their own." That attitude is typical of Rogerian counseling.

Much of what is called "Christian" counseling today is not aimed at bringing Archie to conviction of sin. It is aimed at making him feel better about himself. It neglects the basic reason why a believer must change. A believer must change to please God. Honoring God and His Word, not boosting self-esteem, is the goal of all counseling that is truly biblical. Archie needs to be confronted with his sinful behavior. He needs to understand that he is not only in an unreconciled state with his wife, brother, sister-in-law, and others, but he is in an unreconciled state with God. Any attempt to change Archie without first seeking to restore his relationship with God will result in an outward, pharisaical change.

Archie needs to be rebuked and brought under conviction concerning his attitude toward self-love.

He needs to be taught what Jesus said about self.[16] He must learn that Jesus never commanded His followers to love themselves, esteem themselves, accept themselves, believe in themselves, develop a healthy self-image, or nurture feelings of significance and worth. Rather, He commanded them to deny themselves, esteem others, and seek God first and the good of their neighbor second. The words and actions of our Lord show that He did not teach and model self-love, but instead condemned it.[17]

Archie also needs to be rebuked for his sinful temper[18] and his idleness (the fact that he is not working).[19]

STEP THREE: CORRECTION

To rebuke Archie is to bring a biblical case against him for his sin. It is like a prosecuting attorney who presents evidence against the accused. He tears down the accused person's defenses in order to prove his guilt. Rebuke knocks Archie to the ground, but correction stands him back up again. Jay Adams wrote:

> The Word of God has the positive power of rectifying what has gone wrong. It is able to set straight what has been knocked off base or out of line… The Bible is concerned not only with exposing wrongs, but also

---

[16] Oftentimes rebuking and teaching are done together. In order to rebuke a counselee of his sinful behavior the counselor may have to teach him to think biblically. The counselor may have to clarify certain doctrines that the counselee has misunderstood.

[17] I have written on this topic in my book *Jesus Christ: Self-Denial or Self-Esteem?* In this book I prove that the doctrine of self-love is not taught in the Scripture by using the best example—Christ. I examine Christ's words, miracles, and parables, clearly demonstrating that the proper pattern for life is self-denial.

[18] See Proverbs 14:17, 29; 15:1, 18; 25:28; 29:11, 22.

[19] See 2 Thessalonians 3:6-15; Proverbs 6:6-11; 12:24; 15:19.

with righting them... The Bible boldly
claims to supply what is necessary to help
one change any attitude or behaviors out
of accord with God's will.[20]

The process of correcting our behavior and attitudes
is explained in Ephesians 4 when Paul wrote: **"that, in
reference to your former manner of life** (habits), **you
lay aside the old self, which is being corrupted in
accordance with the lusts of deceit"** (Ephesians 4:22).
Correction means laying aside a sinful practice. However,
laying aside the sinful practice must begin by repenting,
confessing, and seeking the forgiveness of the person
or persons you have offended. Correction must always
include confession of sin and the seeking of forgiveness.

The New Testament word for confession is *homologeo,*
or the more intensive form of the word *exomologeo,* which
means "to say the same thing." It means that when you
have been rebuked and convicted of the error of your
ways you acknowledge your guilt. In other words, you
say the same thing or agree with the rebuke. Archie
needs to confess his sin and guilt and ask forgiveness
of those who have been on the receiving end of his bad
temper. Confession is an important element to biblical
change. There can be no forgiveness and reconciliation
apart from confession of sin.

Further, Archie needs to forsake his sin. Forsaking
sin is the same as putting it off or laying it aside. Putting
off sin is the first step of a two-step process in which the
believer lays aside the old self or sinful habit and puts on
the new self or righteous habit. There is no substitute for

---

[20] Jay Adams, *How to Help People Change* (Grand Rapids: Zondervan Publishing
House, 1986), p. 139.

forsaking our sin. Archie, expressing his enthusiasm to change, says he is willing to do whatever it will take to please God. Some counselees are quick to express their willingness to change, but when they are pressed to go forward and change from their sinful ways, temptations, and stumbling blocks, they draw back. It may be that they are just slow to learn, so the counselor must be patient (2 Timothy 4:2). Some counselees may simply be unwilling to forsake their sin. Since unwillingness to forsake sin is evidence of false repentance, it may be necessary to end counseling with the individual. But this is not the case with Archie.

STEP FOUR: TRAINING IN RIGHTEOUSNESS

Correcting Archie's behavior is not enough. Change requires doing something different. New habits of living must be developed. Laying aside his bad temper is only the first step in the two-step process of putting off sin and putting on righteousness. Archie needs to put off his bad temper by putting on self-control and kindness. Paul said, **"and put on the new self, which in the likeness of God has been created in righteousness and holiness of the truth"** (Ephesians 4:24). In order to make himself more Christ-like Archie needs to renew or change his thinking (Ephesians 4:23). He needs to think biblically. Archie needs to **"set [his] mind on the things above"** (Colossians 3:2). He needs to prepare his mind for action (1 Peter 1:13).

Our failure to change when we want to change can be very discouraging. Archie says he has tried for years to control his temper, but without success. Failure to bring about a change that is permanent is the sad testimony of many Christians who are living in sin. They have been taught doctrine (<u>teach</u>). They have been convicted of sin (<u>rebuke</u>). They know what they need to stop doing and know what they need to do (<u>correction</u>). The problem is they change their ways for a time, but then fall back into the old way of living or habit. Their sanctification is stalled.

Archie's problem, over the years, has been that he has tried to put off his volatile temper, but he has never moved on to the fourth step of "training in righteousness." Archie was taught that **"A hot-tempered man stirs up strife"** (Proverbs 15:18). Archie has been rebuked and convicted of his sin. Archie knows what he needs to be doing. Archie has gotten through teaching, rebuking, and correction, but failed to move on to training in righteousness.

It cannot be emphasized enough. The fourth step is essential to change. To resist change is to grieve the Holy Spirit. Change that sticks is vitally important to the process of sanctification. Sanctification is more than just learning what the Bible teaches about a specific behavior or attitude. Sanctification involves radical and drastic change.[21] Though habits are hard to change they are not impossible to change. Habits are learned and can be unlearned. Personality is not set in stone, but is fluid. Personality can be changed. God changed Jacob into Israel. God changed impetuous and impulsive Simon into Peter, the great preacher of Pentecost. God changed the prideful Saul of Tarsus into Paul, who called himself the chief of all sinners. Archie can change.

---

[21] Many pastors think that directive counseling that insists on radical change must be left to psychiatrists. What they don't realize is psychiatry's beliefs and methods are antithetical to the Scripture. Pastors need to understand that the work of the Holy Spirit, in conjunction with the Scripture, is to change personality. The pastor-counselor is used by the Holy Spirit, as he ministers God's Word, to change people.

Learning the biblical alternatives to the behaviors and attitudes that need to be put off is what correction is about. Archie learned that he needed to "lay aside the old self" or old way of behaving (bad temper). Now Archie must "put on the new self" or new ways (self-control and kindness). That is why Paul said, **"Let him who stole steal no longer, but rather let him labor, working with his hands what is good, that he may have something to share with him who has need"** (Ephesians 4:28). The thief must not only put off stealing (correction), but he must put on or develop the new habits of work and giving (training in righteousness).

True biblical sanctification involves much more than changing a person's behavior. Biblical change is concerned with changing the person. It is a spiritual process that involves three persons: the Holy Spirit, the counselee, and a counselor who will come alongside to minister the Word. The biblical counselor will use Archie's experiences to bring him closer to God. Being "conformed to the image of His Son" is the single most important characteristic of those who change and, therefore, must be the number one factor in counseling.

A biblical counselor is not striving only for change of a behavior or activity. This kind of change occurs under certain conditions and is temporary. The biblical counselor is not so much interested in behavior modification, but in real, substantial change. Heart change is what the biblical counselor aims to achieve. The goal is not merely that Archie will quit blowing up at people, but that Archie himself changes. Archie is not always blowing up, just as a drunkard is not always drunk. Just because Archie is not blowing up *now* or the drunkard is not drunk *now* does not mean there has been change. A pause or break in the sinful activity is not a sign of permanent change. The person himself must change. Jesus said, **"For out of the heart come evil thoughts, murders, adulteries, fornications, thefts, false witness, slanders"** (Matthew 15:19).

Real change means that Archie must be different at the heart level. Training Archie in righteousness has to do with his habits and not with intellectual instruction alone. Habits are comfortable, unconscious, and automatic. For example, Archie said he didn't realize how often he gets angry and blows up.

Paul wrote: **"This I say, and affirm together with the Lord, that you *walk no longer* just as the Gentiles also walk, in the futility of their mind"** (Ephesians 4:17, italics mine). "Walk no longer" is a command to change. Paul was not calling upon believers to give up doing some unacceptable act or deed. Paul was calling on them to change their "manner of life" (Ephesians 4:22). The phrase, "put on a new self," implied the radical characteristics of the change God required (Ephesians 4:24). It was like becoming a new man with a new mind (Ephesians 4:23). Archie must change from being a man with a bad temper, without self-control, into a man with self-control and patience. Jay Adams said,

> Change is a two-factored process. These two factors always must be present in order to effect genuine change. Putting off will not be permanent without putting on. Putting on is hypocritical as well as temporary, unless it is accompanied by putting off.[22]

---

[22] Jay Adams, *The Christian Counselor's Manual* (Grand Rapids: Zondervan Publishing House, 1973), p. 177.

There are many examples of this two-factored process of change. For example, Paul wrote: "**[lay] aside falsehood** (put off)," and "**speak truth each one of you with his neighbor, for we are members of one another** (put on)" (Ephesians 4:25). "**He who steals must steal no longer** (put off); **but rather he must labor, performing with his own hands what is good, so that he will have something to share with one who has need** (put on)" (Ephesians 4:28). "**Let no unwholesome word proceed from your mouth** (put off), **but only such a word as is good for edification according to the need of the moment, so that it will give grace to those who hear** (put on)" (Ephesians 4:29, parenthetical comment mine).[23]

Paul wrote to Timothy: "**But have nothing to do with worldly fables fit only for old women. On the other hand,** *discipline yourself for the purpose of godliness*" (1 Timothy 4:7, italics mine). A person does not become godly by sitting in a pew and absorbing godliness from his environment. A person becomes godly by practicing godliness. Archie put off his uncontrollable temper by putting on self-control. This was done by practice. Archie was not born with a bad temper, but was habituated to it by years of practice. Perhaps it all began when he was a child. He blew up at his brother. Nobody rebuked Archie for his sinful behavior. The next day or the next week Archie blew up at his sister. Each time Archie got his way by getting angry and hollering at others. Eventually, Archie became habituated to solving problems by blowing up. Years later he married his first wife. He blew up at her. They divorced and he married his second wife. He behaved in the same way with her

---

[23] See also Romans 12:14-21; 13:12-14; 1 Corinthians 6:18-20; 7:5; 9:24; 15:33-34; 2 Corinthians 10:5; Galatians 5:19-23; 6:3-4; Ephesians 5:15-17; 6:4; Philippians 2:3-4; 3:13; Hebrews 10:23-25; 1 Peter 1:14-15; 2:11-12; 3:9. This is just a sample list. There are hundreds of put offs and put ons.

too. They divorced and Archie married Edith. Archie behaved toward Edith in the same way he had behaved in the past.

Correction, or making adjustments in one's behavior, is not enough. Unless there is permanent change, Archie will fall back into his old way or habit. Paul was not talking about a superficial change, but in putting off a way of life (Ephesians 4:1, 17, 22-24). **"He who steals"** must change his way of life by putting off idleness and then he **"must labor, performing with his own hands what is good, so that he will have something to share with one who has need"** (Ephesians 4:28). His former manner of life, his habit of stealing, must be replaced with work and sharing with others.

Putting off (correction) will not be permanent without putting on the biblical alternative habit. Archie has complained for years that he has unsuccessfully tried to quit his sins. Will-power and determination are no match for someone who is enslaved to a sin. In cases like Archie's, where a particular sin reigns, deciding not to sin any more is useless without step four. Archie must replace the sinful habit with the righteous habit that pleases God. Only then will he "change."

Habits are learned ways of responding to life's problems and people. Habits are comfortable, automatic, and carried out without conscious thought or decision. Archie was not born with a bad temper; he practiced it until it became a part of him. In the same way righteous habits are acquired through practice. There is no such thing as instant sanctification or godliness. There is no pill or formula for becoming like Christ. Paul wrote to Timothy: **"discipline yourself for the purpose of**

28

godliness" (1 Timothy 4:7). The secret to godliness is discipline. The counselor must help Archie discipline himself for the purpose of godliness. Discipline means work. It means daily effort. It means self-denial. Jesus said to His disciples, **"If anyone wishes to come after Me, he must deny himself, and take up his cross and follow Me"** (Matthew 16:24). Denying himself refers to denying the old desires, ways, or practices. Taking up a cross means death. It means putting to death the old habits of the old man. It means saying no to self every day. But that is not enough. Where there is a putting off in the Scriptures there is also a putting on.

Paul said to Timothy: **"All Scripture is inspired by God and profitable for teaching, for reproof, for correction, for *training in righteousness"*** (2 Timothy 3:16, italics mine). To teach, rebuke, and correct Archie would be insufficient. Archie needs to learn how to live in such a way that he does not fall back into his old ways of living. The Scriptures provide everything necessary to train Archie in righteousness. Training in righteousness is absolutely essential. The counselor must work closely and consistently in order to help Archie practice the desired behavior. It takes four to six weeks of practice to put off a sinful habit and put on the biblical alternative habit.

CONCLUSION

Over the last fifty years, Christians have abandoned their commitment to God's sufficient Word for understanding the nature of man and solving his problems of living. A psychological Tower of Babel has been erected and an era of confusion has ensued. Biblical definitions and categories have changed and a new vocabulary has emerged within the Church. It is the vocabulary of humanistic psychology. Sin is called sickness or low self-esteem. Loving God and neighbor are no longer the first and second commandments. Loving yourself is now the first and greatest commandment. One cannot love anyone else, even God, until he loves himself. Self-esteem is primary.

It is interesting that we hear so much today about the dignity and worthiness of man and so little about his depravity. The biblical idea that man is a sinner has been modified to selfism's concept that man is a "victim." The biblical assertion that man is culpable has been changed to psychology's insistence that man is helpless to stop sinning without raising his self-esteem. The cross, once a symbol of man's wickedness and God's grace, is now said to be "proof" of man's value and worth.

Pride is always inconsistent with the true doctrine of the Gospel. There is nothing more eloquently condemned in Scripture than pride. Any teaching that glorifies man cannot be revealed by God, for He has said that no flesh will glory in His presence. Self-esteem advocates make up an assortment of prides. Among them are good pride, healthy pride, genuine pride, disingenuous pride, sinful pride, etc. And then we are told that it is a terrible thing not to think more highly of ourselves.

Jesus never showed any concern about people having too little self-esteem; therefore, He gave no instructions on how one should enhance self-esteem. He taught and modeled meekness and lowliness. Self has dethroned God and is the new false god. Man loves himself more than anything else. His love for self replaces his love for God. The Apostle Paul wrote,

For even though they knew God, they did not honor Him as God or give thanks, but they became futile in their speculations, and their foolish heart was darkened. Professing to be wise, they became fools, and exchanged the glory of the incorruptible God for an image in the form of corruptible man...For they exchanged the truth of God for a lie, and worshiped and served the creature rather than the Creator, who is blessed forever. Amen (Romans 1:21-25).

Nearly ten weeks after Archie began biblical counseling, he and his counselor mutually decided it was time to terminate the sessions. Archie had reached his goal of learning how to put off his sinful behavior, wrong thinking and attitudes, and put on biblical thinking.

Archie left counseling not merely with a sense of relief that, "at last the problem has been solved," but with joy and thanksgiving. He saw the end of counseling as a new beginning. It was a time for him to make great strides in his Christian faith. He saw it as an opportunity to enter into service for the Lord as never before.

Once Archie saw how biblical counseling had helped him with his problems of wrong thinking, he wanted to help others. Today, Archie and Edith are happily married, and Archie is training to be a biblical counselor.

Further Reading

Jesus Christ: Self Denial or Self-Esteem?   David Tyler

Self-Esteem: Are We Better Than We Think   David Tyler

Psychology As Religion: The Cult of Self-Worship   Paul Vitz

The Danger of Self-Love   Paul Brownback

The Biblical View of Self-Esteem,
Self-Love and Self-Image   Jay Adams

Other Books By David Tyler

God's Funeral:
Psychology—Trading the Sacred for the Secular

Deceptive Diagnosis: When Sin is Called Sickness
(with Kurt Grady)

ADHD: Deceptive Diagnosis (with Kurt Grady)

Available at
www.focuspublishing.com
1.800.913.6287